Talk, Thought, and Thing
the emic road toward conscious knowledge

Talk, Thought, and Thing

the emic road toward conscious knowledge

Kenneth L. Pike
The University of Texas at Arlington
Summer Insitute of Linguistics

Summer Institute of Linguistics
Dallas

Copyright ©1993 by the Summer Institute of Linguistics, Inc.
Library of Congress Catalog Card No. 92-82114
ISBN: 0-88312-610-9

Printed in the United States of America
All Rights Reserved

No part of this publication may be reproduced, stored in a retrieval system, or transmitted in any form or by any means—electronic, mechanical, photocopy, recording or otherwise—without the express permission of the Summer Institute of Linguistics, Inc., with the exception of brief excerpts in magazine articles or reviews.

Cover design by Hazel Shorey

Copies of this and other publications of the Summer Institute of Linguistics may be obtained from:

International Academic Bookstore
7500 West Camp Wisdom Road
Dallas, Texas 75236

Contents

Preface vii

Chapter 1 Personal interaction in a social-physical context is a useful entrance point into theory about cross-cultural knowledge . . 1

Chapter 2 The person, as observer, is tied emically to things (and concepts) via differences, sameness, and appropriateness 15

Chapter 3 The person may react to three kinds of hierarchical structures—phonological, grammatical, and referential—each with its features of slot, class, role, and cohesion 27

Chapter 4 A person chooses temporary perspectives via particle, wave, and field, as a crucial part of the ability of the self . . . 43

Chapter 5 A personal search for knowledge involves the search for patterns within patterns in a holistic context 55

Chapter 6 A person may distort innate positive universals into negative particular action 63

Conclusion 77

Bibliography 79

Preface

This booklet is written for a small number of people unknown to me, who are disillusioned in a changing world. Until recently, mechanistic science as the explanatory source of all social situations and events could seem a sensible position to many young scholars yearning to understand the world of persons as it is. But changing times, changing governments, changing belief systems, make that more difficult now than twenty-five years ago. Somehow, 'people'—irrationally, inconsistently, fighting with guns and minds—seem now to have made choices which add fire to the straw of human plans, programs, and even pleasures.

Where, now, can they turn? Looking in directions dictated by their training, they may see no hope. But where else can they look and not reject their commitment to the validity of science and research? One suggestion, here, is for them to start their research by looking into the nature of language—into language which serves as the 'telephone exchange' of all society and science and which cannot be dropped if one wishes to grow in the knowledge of truth. This, as truth, is not *proven* in this book. On the contrary, it is taken as a *given*, visible to any who wish to look in that direction without demanding a demonstration based upon a proven *logical* starting point.

'We' cannot *start* with logic, unless we *first* have 'ourselves'. A child *is* before it is *grown*. A child trusts its mother—a person must trust in unproven convictions about life before using them to argue about other things. Here we come full circle—from person, to language-in-society, to knowlege, to arguments for validity, and back to the person so arguing. So here I begin with person —but person as interacting through language

Preface

with other persons, along with interaction with things and events in that environment.

Why should I be a person who begins with language? In part because of the inescapableness of language (or, for the mute, with gestures replacing spoken language) and in part for reasons of science. I am a linguist by training and experience—especially with experience in analyzing languages having no alphabet and, therefore, no written documentation of human experience. Yet in these languages we find some of the basic components necessary to a foundation of knowledge based upon experience and a readiness to develop broader concepts built on linguistic metaphor and social analogies appropriate to the highly intellectual competence of, albeit preliterate, peoples.

I have been helped with starting presuppositions, however, by several philosophers —for example, Willard V. Quine, George Mavrodes, and Harry Reeder—which seem to me to range from mechanistic ones, to phenomenological commitment, to theological beliefs. I needed that help, since such logical thinking is not my norm as a descriptive linguist. In addition, I am grateful for editorial or bibliographical help from others —for example from Professor Ruth Brend (linguist) and Dr. Joost Pikkert.

In Chapter one, I discuss the importance of the fact that a language can be learned without the use of an interpreter, and show its relation to the importance of names in categorizing our environment. In Chapter two, sameness, from an insider's point of view, leads to EMIC units (my term invented from PHONEMIC, 1954) with form and meaning tied together. Chapter three suggests three part-whole hierarchies of physical-phonological form, grammatical-sequential presentation of oral material, and background-referential structuring of people and their environments— with each unit of each hierarchy shown as containing elements of position (slot) in context, membership in a substitutable set of items (class), relevance to personal behavior

Preface xi

(role), and control in relation to a background network system (cohesion). These four components are always present in such (tagmemic) units, with kaleidoscopically replaced elements under some conditions. Chapter four shows alternative views of the observer, who may choose to perceive units as static (as particles), as dynamic (as waves), or as systemic (as units placed in a field structure). Chapter five emphasizes the continual presence of a holistic context of pattern within patterns. Chapter six suggests that bad actions are distortions of good types, whether intellectual, aesthetic, physical, social, moral or religious, or in relation to linguistic linking of form to meaning. The final chapter, in summary, emphasizes again that person is more basic than formal logic in language, in life, and in philosophy.

The bibliography is kept relatively small. The book is not an attempt to summarize language research or philosophy as a whole, but refers, in general, only to works which are particularly related to some of the points made here or which can be helpful in understanding them either from supportive or from contrastive points of view.

Kenneth L. Pike
Dallas, Texas, 1992

Chapter 1

Personal interaction in a social-physical context is a useful entrance point into theory about cross-cultural knowledge.

We wish to know about ourselves. We wish to know what we know, and how we know. Are we just minds? Are we just bodies? How are our minds and our bodies connected with our understanding of the world around us?

Conviction 1.1. The knowledge of self, mind, body, and of the world around us, is best understood by starting with it all together, interacting.

The relation of myself to the outside world includes my relation not only to physical elements outside of me, but to minds and language of people outside of me. I suggest, therefore, that our entrance point into an understanding of our knowledge of the world as a whole may best be achieved by looking at the interaction between people within the context of the society around them (which they in part comprise) and within the physical world around them (and of which they also are a part).

Analogy: Language, through which much of the social interchange takes place, may be called a 'telephone exchange' of that society, linking people to each other so that they can all understand each other and, in addition, linking people to their view and knowledge of the physical world.

Source: My viewpoint has grown out of an attempt to understand people cross-culturally, by way of linguistic research across cultures. In order to understand humans, I needed to get beneath physical actions to learn what the purposes of their actions or their beliefs about the environment were. In order to do so, I had to use language. I had to learn to speak a local language, and to listen. But cross-cultural language problems forced me to look at different cross-cultural beliefs about the knowledge of things and thoughts.[1]

Conviction 1.2. In a shared physical-social environment, a person can learn to speak a language without an interpreter. This implies the presence of a shared capacity to learn cross-culturally and to transmit names, social structure, and worldview.

Source: There is an astonishment in watching communication begin under such circumstances. In 1936 I first developed a 'monolingual demonstration' to teach students what they could do if they were trying to learn a language in some area where there

---

[1]Compare, also, Reeder 1986:123, where "the phenomenology of language" begins "with analysis of the meaning-intention, that is, the intentional experience of meaningful language use."

is no alphabet, no dictionary, no written grammar, and no interpreter available to them. I meet the person on a platform in front of the students (or others) without knowing what the language is, nor where the person comes from. Members of the faculty pick him or her for the occasion, without telling me where he or she comes from. With a few leaves, sticks, stones, or other items, I start pointing at one of those items and can usually expect the other person to reply (in his or her language unknown to me) with some such statement as "that is a stick." Usually, within a half hour, I have the names for a dozen objects or so, plus a few size differences ('big leaf' versus 'little leaf'), a few numbers ('two leaves'), or sentences such as 'He hit me with a stick' versus 'I hit him with a stick'. Occasionally, however, it takes much longer than that to get started. In one instance, in Australia, an aboriginal speaker waited about five minutes before he would utter a single syllable or give a single word. I learned later that the speaker did this because, in his village, it was not polite for an outsider to begin talking immediately. He first needed to be interviewed by an old man of the area to see who his ancestors or relatives were and to whom he could talk politely without social taboos. Nevertheless, the demonstration did get under way. In any one instance, it is always possible that one might fail in such a short period of time.

I developed this monolingual demonstration because I was (and for half a century since have been) involved in training students to work in the analysis of unwritten languages around the world. I could not have worked happily or successfully without some of these presuppositions either implicit or explicit.

Further Implications: Strong support for the relevance of naming, in a monolingual situation, comes from two philosophers. Quine (who, I have been told, is the leading living American philosopher) has discussed the implications of this kind of demonstration for over two decades. In Quine 1960:40-45, he called utterances obtained by pointing at something in this kind of a demonstration

OBSERVATION SENTENCES.[2] Ullian joins with Quine to give extraordinarily strong support for the relevance of these utterances, stating that "observation sentences are at the bottom edge of language . . . It is ultimately through them that language gets its meaning, its bearing on reality. This is why it is they that convey the basic evidence for all belief, all scientific theory" (Quine and Ullian 1978:28).

One advantage to insisting on the importance of a monolingual demonstration is that it begins with intersubjectivity, with people working together; but in addition it ties people and things into a package as a starting point. It thus rejects the possibility of starting with abstract minds without reference to the physical world. And, similarly, it rejects the possibility of beginning philosophically with the minimum units of the physical world which may be inaccessible to us in terms of common sense experience. So our monolingual demonstration experience is important as being possible—and it delays

---

[2] See also Quine 1974:37-41.

the necessity for the discussion of ultimate starting points if they are to be stated in terms of presuppositions from mechanism, theism, pantheism, animism, or other postulated sources. It begins with the possibility and relevance of human behavior in physical context.

Analogy: The shared language capacity in human nature can be looked at as *hardware:* the learned specifics of a different language may be considered its *software.*

Conviction 1.3. For some purposes it is better to start from a complex situation and to work towards simplicity, rather than trying to start from simplicity and work to the complex.

Analogy: If one wishes to understand an automobile, it may be helpful to start by learning to drive one and by using it to go buy groceries, rather than to start by studying the structure of one bolt in one wheel. Similarly, if we wish to understand a 'homerun' in baseball, we need to see two teams in interaction trying to 'win' a game. To begin with an analysis of the leather on the baseball itself would not lead us to play the game quickly and easily. Similarly, for a native speaker of English to study English by itself is insufficient training for studying an unwritten language abroad. One needs to get farther away from 'home base'!

Conviction 1.4. Normal human nature requires the naming and discussion of things, events, ideas, and persons.

Analogy: A shepherd dog must be able to distinguish a sheep from a horse, to function normally. An adult person, however, needs words to discuss the difference in meaning between the phrases *ancient and elegant,* and *modern and garish.*

Further Implications: In the physical sciences, a categorization in the ordinary sense is also basic. We cannot start a scientific discussion without first having an experience of common sense discussion of things and events and people. The physicist Einstein (in Samuel 1952:158) said:

"The most elementary concept in everyday thought, belonging to the 'real,' is the concept of continually existing objects, like the table in my room. The table as such, however, is not given to me, but merely a complex of sensations is given to which I attribute the name and concept 'table'." Also note the philosopher Searle (1984:78): "For a large number of social and psychological phenomena the concept that names the phenomenon is itself a constituent of the phenomenon."

Conviction 1.5. Names and statements are used to link person to person in speech.

Source: An anthropologist talking to another anthropologist about an ancient civilization needs, also, to be able to refer to bones or stones. Both science and society need naming.

Analogy: We must be able to say whether the truck hit the bicycle or the bicycle hit the truck. And we must be able to say that Susan was the grandmother of Sally or was her granddaughter.

Conviction 1.6. This entrance point allows us to begin with a philosophical context which we can 'live in' as well as 'think by'.

Analogy: If I want to build a house I can live in for the next few years, I do not start by collecting separate molecules.

Source: As I have indicated above, I am starting from linguistic experience, working with preliterate language communities, and teaching others to build a 'literate house' for such a society. I start by feeling these components strongly, not by proving them philosophically. It is here that experience of a particular type has had strong influence on shaping my approach.

Conviction 1.7. Approximate translation is possible; it may be viewed as a variety of cross-cultural paraphrase.

Chapter 1

In the monolingual demonstration referred to above, problems arise. I may point to something that I myself am thinking of as a 'stick' but get a reply that it is a 'twig'. This is an approximation toward the translation sought, but not total isomorphism because size was not taken into account. The speaker and hearer may agree, under appropriate circumstances, that two different statements are 'saying the same thing' relative to the purpose of the speaker, the expectations of the hearer, and the shared cultural horizon. But for either paraphrase or translation, identity of words is unnecessary, identity of particular grammatical focal mechanism is unnecessary, and the exact same degree of detail is unnecessary. Truth, in such a statement, is not dependent upon the exact degree of precision obtained, if the generalizations are acceptable to both speaker and hearer. Difficulties in understanding—and hence in paraphrasing or translating—may be especially prominent where substantial ambiguity (or range of meaning) is present in the initial statement. Under such circumstances, the hearer may request further detail or may specifically ask which of two alternatives is involved.

Analogy: On a trip to Pluto, someone might say, 'Are we landing?'—and one paraphrase could be, 'Are we going to land on Pluto?' But another person could say, 'Are we in the process of moving downward?' Knowing what is wanted may result in alternative paraphrases—or translations—to reach those objectives.

Source: Here, again, we rely on our linguistic experience as the source of our opinions. Multiple alternative translations are possible from one language to another, with different emphases—each translation varying with the translator's interpretation of the original author's focus and with each translation requiring different background information to be made explicit for the translation to be intelligible.

Further Implications: As I have stated elsewhere (Pike 1982:15), "Identity of a talk-concept referential unit is specified for a particular time and situation by paraphrase, that is, by the ability to say the same thing in other ways which the hearer and speaker can agree on as being the same concept for their joint temporary purposes." An instructor may ask a student to put 'in his own words' that which the instructor has been saying. The instructor may approve the student's attempt, even though no two words are repeated, if there is no clash with content or with coherence with background. Identity of words is not necessary; identity of a particular grammatical focus mechanism is not necessary; exactly the same degree of detail is not necessary. Truth, in such a summary statement, is not dependent upon the exact degree of precision obtained if the generalizations are acceptable (Pike 1961:3f); but coherence with background pattern expressed, implicit or intended, must not be lost. Expectancies of the hearer must be met by the speaker, with a degree of coherence with reality as perceived by the speaker, for such a paraphrase to be acceptable.

Exceptions to the possibility of specific translation are discussed by Catford (1965: 98–103), in instances where linguistic ambiguity is involved and where this ambiguity is utilized by the speaker as part of his presentation. Puns, for example, cannot normally be translated directly by puns in the target language. They can be explained, but the explanation of a pun does not carry the same impact as the pun itself—an impact which in tagmemic theory is part of the meaning.[3]

---

[3]Further problems in translation—for example seeking for dynamic translatability—can be found in Nida and Tabor 1969:22–24; see also Larson 1984.

Chapter 2

The person, as observer, is tied emically to things (and concepts) via differences, sameness, and appropriateness.

Conviction 2.1. For the native observer within a particular culture, emic units are considered to differ from one another in relation to everyday behavior.

Analogy: A boy is not a girl. A mountain is not a valley. Yesterday, viewed from now, is not today. Youth is not age. Emic units contrast. The contrast between the two vowels in *bit* and *bet*, in English, makes them emically different (called phonemically different when sounds of language are under discussion).

Source: I coined the term EMIC (in Pike 1954) from the linguistic term PHONEMIC, to apply to contrastive items of nonphonological material rather than just to phonological data. It is easy for us to differentiate an airplane from a wheelbarrow. But it is not easy for some of us to differentiate a copperhead snake from a rattler, even though it may be simple for people who are used to avoiding the both of them. They need to be seen as emically different, for survival, in some contexts.

Further Implications: Several years ago when I was lecturing to the philosophy club at the University of Texas at Arlington, a phenomenologist, Professor Lenore Langsdorf, said to me, "You sound like Immanuel Kant." I was surprised. I had not thought of that—but on checking it I found that my linking of observer to thing has some overlap with Kant in thought. Kant says (1966:70),

"We can attain to a knowledge of appearances only, never to that of the things in themselves." I would agree that there is no way to completely eliminate our own observer impact on our own relation to the universe. Our categorization of elements of our universe allows us to have a partial understanding of the universe. As we categorize it, we *turn it into* things *as if* they are isolable or recurrent, even though they can never occur outside of some kind of physical or mental context. Units resulting from such categorization I call EMIC UNITS.[4] Years ago (1957), a philosopher in Spain, Ortega y Gasset, adopted Kant's viewpoint, and developed it in detail.[5]

Conviction 2.2. Any theory which we can *live by* must be able to grant that *insiders* to a system (such as the native speakers of a

---

[4]And note that such categorization may be called 'naming' as in *Convictions* 1:4–5.

[5]See his revision (Ortega y Gasset 1985: 232). It is the thing within our lives, not the thing in itself, which he considered important. Note, also, related items on pp. 44f, 163, 173, 196f, 201f, 230.

language) may call or treat several items or concepts as *the same* even though outside analysts may notice differences between them. This is EMIC SAMENESS in the face of ETIC DIVERGENCE. In some instances the insider responds so strongly to the sameness that it may take special training for him or her to recognize differences. In others, the differences may be obvious but ignored, as irrelevant to the communicative purpose of the speaker.[6]

Source: It was with astonishment, years ago, that I learned that the two *p*-sounds of the word *paper* are different in my own dialect of English—the first is aspirated (pronounced with a tiny puff of breath following it), but the second is unaspirated. The sameness was for me *emic* (phonemic); I had not observed the *etic* difference until I

---

[6]Emically, I would say, one can step into Heraclitus' river twice, but etically it will be a different river each time because, he says (Frost 1962:8), "You could not step into the same river twice, for other and yet other waters are ever flowing on"—with different molecules each time.

had studied some phonetics. On the other hand, with the concept 'house', I had no difficulty in calling a big house and a little house by the same term. The sensitivity to the etic variability or spread of applicability in the second case was much broader than in the first. The variability within sameness may be easier for the insider to recognize in relation to nonphonological items and behavior than it is within phonology.[7]

Further Implications: For reading on the importance of the distinction between EMIC and ETIC from contrastive viewpoints (with synchronic focus versus diachronic focus), see Headland, Pike, and Harris 1990.

Conviction 2.3. Emic difference is easier to detect when two somewhat similar items occur appropriately in the same position in a typical sequence of behavior, but where the two items are perceived by the insider as implying significantly different meanings

---

[7]See *Conviction 4:5* below, for a discussion of WAVE.

or behavioral relevance. Emic contrasts—emic differences—occur in appropriate places in sequential behavior or in a systemic arrangement.

Emic units relevant to behavior occur in contrastive positions in that behavior. The sounds *p* and *t* contrast (phonemically, and hence emically) at the beginning of the words *pie* and *tie*, but the two *ps* of *paper*, although different (phonetically, and hence etically), occur in different positions in the word and are sufficiently alike to be ignored in relation to semantic relevance. On the other hand, if one says the same word *pie* a thousand times, a machine can register slight differences in each of the pronunciations. These differences are etic variants which do not carry semantic implications. Occasionally further problems arise, as when a person can have two emically different pronunciations of the same word. His colleagues know that they are different, but they can know that difference because the sounds are contrastive in other circumstances.

He may say "I am going," rapidly, as "I'm going."[8]

Analogy: A pancake is not a hot dog; they contrast emically in our culture. But a pancake may be relatively thick or relatively thin and still be a pancake. In my youth, a pancake would have been more appropriate at breakfast, whereas a hot dog would have been more appropriate for lunch or supper.

Conviction 2.4. Both the physical form of an item or action and its social meaning or impact comprise parts of an emic unit. The observer, therefore, is involved in the contrastive categorization of the environment, even in those instances in which there is physical isomorphism between two emically contrastive units.

---

[8]Methodological difficulties arise in applying these criteria, but they are not appropriate to the discussion here. For my earlier discussion of this methodology, see Pike 1947a.

Analogy: A person may kill someone by hitting him with an automobile. A second person may do likewise. But if the first person did it unintentionally, that social component helps categorize the incident as an ACCIDENT; but if it was done intentionally by the second person, that would be categorized as MURDER. Courts of law, therefore, in this kind of situation, try to investigate not only the physical facts, but also the mental involvement of the actors and the observer interpretation or evaluation of intents, lying behind the observed actions. All of these are a part of the emic categorization.

Further Implications: For the necessity of both form and meaning, discussed in relation to tagmemic principles, see Pike 1982: 109–17.

Conviction 2.5. I reject, therefore, as not being an interpretation of life which I can in fact live by, an analysis which treats human behavior exclusively in relation to mental components of an individual. I also reject, for my purposes, any analysis which treats all of behavior as exclusively physical. Similarly, I must reject an analysis of behavior which separates mental and physical so sharply that they fail to take account of their observable overlap when the observer acts to categorize his environment emically.

Analogy: In (1a), I draw two circles, completely separated from each other, and label the first circle 'ideas' and the second one 'physical action'. This implies two kinds of activity, but leaves them totally separate. Then, in (1b), a single circle represents only ideas, with no physical action believed in. (1c) does the opposite, with only physical action, without ideas. All of these I reject. In figure (1d), however, the partial separation plus partial overlap suggests the kind of view I hold, where self and body are in part overlapping and in part distinct.

Source: The observer names material and, in thus categorizing his environment, in part gets to know his environment; and he or she in part creates for his or her own mental and social activity the emic categorization of that environment. This viewpoint seems to me to leave better room for the SELF (or soul) to exist along with body, not as merely a part of it (see chapter 4).

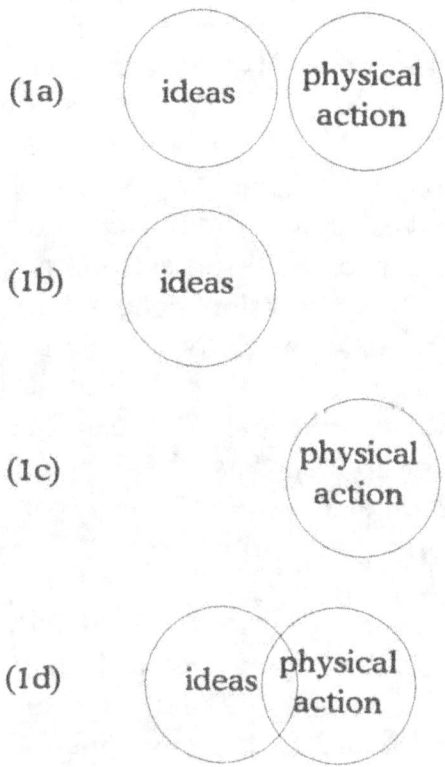

Chapter 2

Further Implications: I had supposed (without pondering deeply upon the problem) that when I wrote and published my book on phonemics (1947a) that I was doing it from a mechanistic perspective. I was startled, therefore, to receive a letter from Czechoslovakia saying that they were delighted to see my book, after having seen mechanistic material from the Yale school. I asked myself how they could have known I was not philosophically a mechanist even though I had thought that I was writing as one. I decided, later, that it must have been because I insisted so strongly, without discussing the underlying philosophical reasons for it, that the native speaker had reactions of understanding or of identity or of difference which were relevant to the methodology of analysis. See, for example, Pike 1947a:64 (and cf. 160), with 'native reaction' as a source of my premises: We want the student "to arrive at an analysis which parallels the vague or explicit observable reactions of speakers to their own sounds"; and "the observation that speakers of English have difficulty in learning to distinguish between the two [p] sounds in 'paper' leads to the conclusion that in some way the sounds are 'the same' for them."

Chapter 3

The person may react to three kinds of hierarchical structures—phonological, grammatical, and referential—each with its features of slot, class, role, and cohesion.

Cultural categories involve different kinds of hierarchies. One of these is the part-whole hierarchy. (The nose is part of the face. The face is part of the body.) On the other hand, a taxonomic hierarchy identifies an item as a member of a class of classes of items. (A dog is a whole animal. An animal is a whole kind of thing. But a nose is not a whole human body.)

Conviction 3.1. In language, there are three different kinds of interlocking, part-whole hierarchies: grammatical, phonological, and referential.

The grammatical hierarchy deals with conversational structure, with monologues broken into paragraphs, with sentences broken into clauses, with phrases broken into words, and with sequences of morphemes broken into single morphemes. The word *boys*, for example, is broken into the two morphemes *boy* and *s*. Grammatical structuring involves such units, in some kind of sequence. The sequence may be called THE ORDER OF TELLING of a narrative (or of the presenting of another kind of nonnarrative discourse). Phonological structure deals with the physical components of sound as speakers and hearers respond to them emically. This hierarchy can include, for example, the phonological structure of a poem with its rhyme and other factors, the grouping of material in a sentence or part of a sentence by intonation, the rhythmic grouping of syllables surrounding a stressed syllable, the individual syllable, or the sounds making up a syllable.[9] Referential structure involves the order and social or physical structuring of a HAPPENING. In *John went to the movies, after he came home and had eaten supper*, for example, the happening sequence is that John first came home, then ate supper, then went to the movies; and the referential structure also includes the unstated structuring of his home in geographic relation to the movie theater. Referential also includes the taxonomic structure, for example, of a kinship system.

Source: A linguistic reason for assuming three part-whole hierarchies, in tagmemic theory, is that units of the three are sometimes nonisomorphic. Since units from the three hierarchies are present in some way in every utterance, only one hierarchy would be needed if units from each of the three always began and ended at the same points.

---

[9]Not under discussion here is the fact that it can include important changes of voice quality and the features which emically differentiate one sound from another.

But the opposite is the case. In *I'm going*, for example, *I'm* is a single syllable but includes part of two grammatical units, the pronoun *I*, and the verb phrase *am going*. Nonisomorphism between grammar and reference is seen in the illustration of reference above, where the referential sequence is John first coming home, then eating supper, then going to the movies; but the event is presented grammatically with the first clause as *John went to the movies*, followed by *after he came home*.

Conviction 3.2. Tagmemic units at any level of any of the hierarchies have features of CLASS (set membership) and SLOT (position in the structure) which in part are reciprocally definable.

Source: To know what a noun phrase is in English, for example, we need to know that it is one of a set of items which could fill a position of subject, or of object, in a normal clause such as *The boy saw the tiger*. Other noun phrases could fill those positions, as in *Several persons located the*

Chapter 3

appropriate house. The total class (set) of such elements in those positions helps define noun phrase. On the other hand, the concept of object in those clauses (the slot or position) is in part determined, in analysis, by the fact that those classes can occupy that position. These two characteristics of slot and class help define the tagmemic unit of object which can be filled, for example, by a noun phrase. A subject slot may likewise be so filled.

Conviction 3.3. A tagmemic unit, as part of a stream of speech, also has a third feature in communication, a feature of role (or relevance, or purpose, or cause).

Source: This conviction grows out of the 'obvious' experience of seeing that the function of a subject in English is not the same as that of an object in a clause such as those quoted. Note, further, that there is non-isomorphism between role and position, and that this forces the latter to be treated as emically distinct. For example, the subject in *John shot the tiger* and the subject in *The tiger was shot by John* are quite different, as ACTOR versus UNDERGOER of that action. This role difference of the two contrastive subject types helps to define the difference between an active and a passive clause.

Note further that slot, class, and role are also relevant to nonverbal behavior. On a football team, the quarterback plays in a limited physical position (slot) behind the linesmen and has a distinct function (role) among the offensive players of throwing the ball or calling the signals; and there is just one member of the quarterback class of that team on the field at any given time (whereas there are several other members of the team who are linesmen). Such features help to define all kinds of relevant (emic) human behavior in all kinds of environments.

Note that in discussing physical events within a society, the role of an actor could be his intention or purpose. In an American court of law, for example, a verdict may depend upon the jury's decision as to whether or not a person intended to kill someone else, or whether it was an accident which he tried to avoid. Our interpretation of such events cannot be autonomous in relation to our beliefs or judgments or guesses about the purposes of the people acting. Similarly, we must be able to guess at physical causes for certain kinds of events —we may guess that a thunderstorm caused the electricity to be interrupted in our house —and take appropriate action.

Intentions or wishes can be made explicit in a sentence like *I wish you would close the door*. Or they can be made implicit in a statement like *The door is open, and I am shivering*, where the hearer knows (by deduction or experience) that the speaker wants him to close the door. Nonverbal actions can also express such intentions. The actor above, for example, could pretend to shiver strongly, and then gesture toward the door. In some instances, a speaker may lie about his intentions or be confused. Nevertheless, the importance of implicit as well as explicit intent, purpose, and cause must be taken into account.

Further Implications: Note, for example, comments from Searle (1984:26): "On my view the mind and the body interact, but they are not two different things, since mental phenomena are just features of the brain." And (27) "There really are mental states; some of them are conscious; many have intentionality; they all have subjectivity; and many of them function causally in determining physical events in the world . . . Naive mentalism and naive physicalism are perfectly consistent with each other. Indeed, as far as we know anything about how the world works, they are not only consistent, they are both true."

Conviction 3.4. Every tagmemic unit has a fourth feature—either an implicit or, occasionally, an explicit relation to the background social, physical, and mental structure against which it occurs, which controls it, or which determines part of the potential, legitimate interpretation of the event under discussion. In tagmemics we call this COHESION; others might refer to it as FRAME

Chapter 3   35

OF REFERENCE; or, as in phenomenology, HORIZON.[10]

Source: The relevance of the sentence *John died today*, is not known unless we also know that 'John' is father, or brother, or son of the speaker, or that he is a member of the same championship football team. And, as for the earlier mention of judgment in a court of law *(Conviction 2.4)*, we need to know background material affecting the event: was the car defective, with poor brakes (which the driver knew or did not know about)? If we hear the phrase *Congratulations, John!*, we need to know

---

[10]For the latter, the philosopher Ricoeur states (in Bien 1978:125): "By context we mean not only the linguistic environment of the actual words, but the speaker's and the hearer's behavior, the situation common to both and finally the horizon of reality surrounding the speech situation." The ability to focus on differing aspects of an event are part of the philosophy adopted by Husserl, as explained by Reeder (1986:11), where the meaning as a whole may have a very different texture or gestalt, and the focus may differ from the horizon.

whether John has just been elected to an important position, has just received a prize, or has just gotten married.

In grammar, cohesion may control agreement—as when a plural noun subject requires a plural verb in *The boys are singing*. In phonology, a poem of a certain structure may require a particular pattern of rhyming, as in the last two lines of a limerick. In discussing family relations, we may normally assume that parents will be exerting a considerable amount of control over the activities of a three-year-old boy, and that they will be doing so generally—beyond any one particular instance.

The four features of slot, class, role, and cohesion may put people into a single graph structure, as in (2). A four-cell tagmeme includes four kinds of contexts—occurrence in a particular structural position, occurrence in a particular replaceable set of items, occurrence in relation to intent or cause, and occurrence in relation to a background system (or frame of reference, or horizon). In a grammatical or phonological slot, occurrence

(2) Where?   What?
    SLOT   CLASS
    (structural position)   (paradigmatic set)

    Why?   How controlled?
    ROLE   COHESION
    (pragmatic intent   (systemic background,
    or cause)   or frame of reference,
                        or horizon)

is in terms of syntagmatic arrangement or sequence of the moment. In class, it is one item replaceable by others (paradigmatically). For role, there is pragmatic relevance to human behavior. For cohesion, there is systematic relation to *n*-dimensional behavioral, physical, or social space. Such a graph shows a human being interacting with the language or the event or the situation being described. And for cohesion, the system is shown as an *n*-dimensional space.

Conviction 3.5. Human nature requires that something from slot, class, role, and cohesion always be available in all speech. Hence, if one of the cells of slot, role, or cohesion has something moved from it and placed into the class cell as a grammatical topic of discussion, something else must then take the place of the item removed from that other cell.

Analogy: Consider a kaleidoscope as a tube containing three mirrors along its sides, plus an end compartment with small bits of colored glass. When the tube is turned, the bits and pieces of glass in sight are not always the same, others come into sight at the turn of the tube, and the pattern of bits of glass seen through the tube varies. In speech, the analog to the bits of glass are the bits of knowledge available in the cohesion background. The new topic, chosen to fill the cell for grammatical class, may be taken, for example, from some hitherto unstated part of the background cohesion cell or the purpose of the event may be chosen as the focus— especially, if the speaker chooses to discuss for example, lying or puns.

Source: For some years I have been trying experiments with syntax, to see how rearrangement of material in a text could be handled, and how it affected the grammar. Eventually (Pike 1988) I took a short poem of mine, and retold it in a number of different ways, changing attention from the event, to the time, or to its place, or to the purpose, or to a higher level in the structure of the background event. To my astonishment, whenever I took something from the slot or role cells and placed it under grammatical focus in the class cell, some other kind of slot, position, or role immediately filled the cell from which the focused element was taken.

In (3) I present a different poem of mine discussing the sadness of a person in a society which has no alphabet, but where the result is social ostracism and a feeling of being noncivilized. Emphasis is on the fact that the lack of an alphabet makes a person feel isolated and damaged in a larger literate society of the world of which he is a part.

(3) **Who Cares**
Mother named me;
Culture maimed me.
Alphabet none;
Socially alone.
Who cares!

SLOT (position) CLASS (topic)
= Alone = Person without alphabet

ROLE (result) COHESION (background)
= Maimed = In a society in the world

Another poem in (4) focuses on the pain implicit in the first poem, and hence I put the pain in the cell for class. It then changes the role from maiming, as such, to the damage to the soul—by way of shame. The background (referential) social situation remains unchanged, as the (referential) controlling source of the social problem.

(4)   **Pain from Alphabet Lack**
*Soul-shame
Maiming is paining,
Grown in vacuum
Of preliterate lack
Of social credit-rating.*

SLOT (position)   CLASS (topic)
  In cultural vacuum   Pain maims
ROLE (result)   COHESION (background)
  Soul shame   In a society in the world

Further Implications: Knowledge, from this emic point of view, is known in relation to the three hierarchies of phonology, grammar, and reference, and in relation to the features of the tagmemic units at each level, via contexts of slot, class, role, and cohesion. The phonological structure in hierarchical detail is also easily illustrated by the analysis of poems. For a detailed example, see Pike and Pike 1983:74–103, where a poem by Langston Hughes is analyzed in terms of the syllable, the phonological phrase structure, and the phonological structure of the poem as a whole. The analysis is related to the phonological characteristics of the poem as read by Ossie Davis (not merely to the written form of the poem). At each level, the units are described in terms of slot, class, role, and cohesion. One can see there that its phonological structure is made up of sounds and syllables, which group into larger rhythmic patterns. In addition, there is a simultaneous structuring of rhyming lines built into structured stanzas. There is also the further structuring of voice quality and of the general speed which affect stanzas as wholes. Beyond that, superimposed upon it, is the important, meaningful intonational form of the pitch of the voice.

Chapter 4

A person chooses temporary perspectives via particle, wave, and field, as a crucial part of the ability of the self.

Conviction 4.1. To serve numerous human purposes, a person needs a self, beyond muscle and physical brain, to choose the direction of his or her internal rudder.

Analogy: A ship needs a pilot. Without the pilot, the ship cannot serve numerous ports.

Source: I hold this conviction unproven, as a presupposition including a nonphysical self in addition to the physical brain. Thus I have chosen to start with postulates which begin with the validity of person, including the person as having genuine choice in some areas, at some times, to some degree. I include the ability to make choices as part of my own epistemological component; without it, I would find it difficult to explain why I have chosen to write this book.

Conviction 4.2. If we must put person in a context along with logic, I would put the value of person above that of logic. Our basic, unproven presuppositions do not come from logic itself, but from persons living in society and in the physical world.

Source: Logic, by itself, can never determine that anything is ultimately true, since logic requires starting presuppositions which are accepted as true by persons—and eventually some of those propositions are unprovable by that person. He starts by believing them. I accepted this assumption many years ago, based on discussions with the philosopher Sinclair.[11]

Conviction 4.3. Poetry is a linguistic device which sometimes goes BEHIND or BEYOND logic to personal feelings which grapple with or accept these unproven presuppositions. Poetry—and other linguistic components of speech—relies heavily on metaphor (or parable, or folk tale) chosen to illustrate, or to support, or in part to develop further an understanding of the internal nature of such presuppositions.

Source: Poetry, folk tales, and metaphor seem to me to have been used for such purposes at least as long as humans have used a more formal logic. These linguistic devices are not irrelevant. They help to capture the way human nature operates.

Analogy: Two of my own poems discussing this problem are presented as (5) and (6).

---

[11]See also Sinclair 1951.

(5) **Logic Needs Person**

Wells run dry
 With no springs below.
Logic fails
 With no chosen start.
Believe, to see—
 Lest doubt run blind.

(6) **Foundations**

Science will sink,
With no ocean to swim in.
"What ocean?" says you.
The ocean of faith's foundations.
 Belief is not 'residue'
 After science has swum away.
 It is the sustaining, undergrounding
 Soul of thought.

My assumption, therefore, is that these convictions grow from the relationship of person to society and to the physical world, not from logic alone.

Chapter 4

Conviction 4.4. The self can choose to focus attention on emic things or events, or on situations, or even on persons, AS IF they were semi-isolable chunks—that is, as static particles.

Source: Perhaps our most normal or frequent way of looking at things or events is to see them as if they begin and end—almost, as it were, as if they were isolated from their context for that moment. We may look at a child as if AT THIS MOMENT it is in some sense a totality, a thing; we do this even though we know from internal knowledge that the child is growing. If we were to fail to do this, we would be unable to speak to the child as if he or she is something that we could now talk to, think about, plan with, or give orders or encouragement to. Similarly, it would be impossible to conduct ordinary affairs if we could not, for example, buy a house as if it were not something there which could be looked at, walked into, and treated as some kind of totality in semi-autonomy from the past and future. Even ideas, also, can be treated as if tentatively FIXED at some point, in so far as discussion is concerned. If this were not true, we could not argue easily about who is right about some concept under discussion. And in a physical sense, a person may choose to look one moment in one direction, and in another moment in another direction, to fix focus on one or another object. In using language, also, we may think that particular sentences in fact may begin or end, or that particular words are accessible to us, or—under a special kind of attention—that a word like jump is made up of separable bits of sounds written as j, u, m, p. Without this concept of language for at least part of the time, we could not either begin—or end—a conversation.

Conviction 4.5. A person can choose to focus attention on the same emic things, or events, or situations, or persons, as if they were in a sequence with indeterminate borders—as sequential DYNAMIC WAVES—but with attention often placed on their central, or most important, components, their nuclei.

Or the waves may be circular, intersecting in (regular or irregular) Venn diagrams.[12]

Source: A person may temporarily operate under a perspective of treating all events or items as processes of activities—waves—which emerge from their environment gradually and merge back into it gradually, with smearing from one point to the other as the activities of various things overlap in time. A house, when being looked at for purchase, may be of interest to the potential purchaser because it is *just getting finished* or may be rejected because it is *tumbling down*. And in terms of the sounds of language, I said years ago (1943:107) that "a SEGMENT is a sound ... having indefinite borders but with a center that is produced by a crest or trough of stricture during the even motion or pressure of an initiator." There are not sharp breaks between the sounds of speech. There is

---

[12]The term VENN DIAGRAM, as stated in a dictionary of philosophy by Flew (1979:340), grows out of work in 1880 by the English logician John Venn, discussing logic diagrams for syllogisms.

overlap from one to the other in the sequence: in the word *June* the lips are more rounded for the *n* than they are for the *n* in *Jan* because the rounding formation of the lips for the vowel of the first carries over to its final consonant. If we fail to grant validity to a wave view for certain purposes, even though balanced by a particle view, we would be unable to operate under certain normal human circumstances. We would be unable to recognize a woman, after she had waved her hair.

In some instances, however, the overlap would seem to be like a pond in which someone has tossed, at the same moment, several different pebbles—and the ripples come together in an irregular pattern. In semantics, a complex illustration might show the overlapping contexts and meanings of the verb *run*, in various contexts, as in *the boy ran fast, he ran the business into the ground, there was a run in my stocking, he was run ragged.*

Conviction 4.6. The self can also choose to focus attention on these same events, or

Chapter 4

emic items, or situations, or persons, as if they were points in an emic system, that is, in a RELATIONAL FIELD.

Source: Life is not merely a sensing of a sequence of bits and pieces, or of things under change, but includes the perception of those items as points in a larger structured context, a FIELD. The points in such a field have RELATIONSHIP one to another, and those relationships help define the units themselves, which are made up of CONTRASTIVE FEATURES which help to identify one unit from another. In themselves, the relationships form a pattern of contrastive features. A phonetic chart represents one such system of units classified by features. Columns may indicate respectively lips, tongue tip, or back of tongue (as for [p], [t], [k]). The rows may reflect complete interruption of voice (as STOPS), or continuing friction, or air escaping from the nose (as [p] versus [f] versus [m]). A house, in turn, may be studied by a purchaser in reference to its floor plan—its field structure. The purchaser may wish to get into the kitchen without going with muddy feet through the living room; she wants to know the floor plan, its field structure. And in order to understand a person's philosophical viewpoint, one appreciates knowing how he or she fits in an academic discipline—as mechanist or idealist—so that the person can be seen in relation to the structure of the discipline. In politics, we cannot understand the action of the government under stress unless we know something of the economic structure of that government. For such purposes, we need to have clearly in mind the intersection of the contrastive features which help determine the relevance of possible actions and persons under those circumstances, and to understand their purposes, or that of their colleagues, or neighbors, or enemies.

The handling of the contrastive features of the sounds of a language, as seen in a phonetic chart, however, is a development of generations of prior scholars. Thus, the idea of static, dynamic, and relational ways of looking at data is not new. It represents experience over historical time, as the experience of a child grows to be that of an adult, or as an adult becomes an analytical scholar. A different statement, however, must be made about the specific source of my use of the terms particle, wave, and field. In the 1950s, out of a general interest in science, I was reading a book by Einstein and Infeld (1938). I was astonished to find that many of their problems, which they treated in relation to physics, seemed to me to have analogies in my own focus on linguistic structure. So, when I was requested to write an article about linguistics for the general academic community, I chose to use them as a metaphor, in an article (1959) entitled "Language as Particle, Wave, and Field." The terms proved to be so useful there that I later adopted them for much of my normal linguistic, anthropological, and sociolinguistic discussion.

The use of the terms to link my personal focus not only on language structure, but also on society and on the physical universe, seemed a bit strange for a while. It became astonishingly appropriate, however, when I read in the work of Bruner (1974:24) that

Niels Bohr, physicist, had developed the principles of complementarity—which he labeled particle, wave, and field—in relation to his own personal family situation. Bohr had to punish his son, but he asked himself, "could he, constrained both by his duty as father and by his fondness for his son, know his son simultaneously both in the light of love and in the light of justice?" And I, then, told myself that if the complementarity of particle, wave, and field grew out of Bohr's social family problem, it was also appropriate that I should use those terms to cover my linguistic needs, social needs, and relation to components of the physical world. (This may prove to have been one of the most important decisions of my academic struggle.)

Chapter 5

A personal search for knowledge involves the search for patterns within patterns in a holistic context.

No pattern can occur in isolation, autonomous from a larger kind of context or set of assumptions, and still be meaningful to human beings. Patterns require larger contexts, with relevance to more inclusive patterns, if they are themselves to be meaningful to us. The total autonomy of parts of knowledge does not exist.

Conviction 5.1. A description of units within patterns within larger intersecting patterns is a kind of knowledge and a component of truth.

Source: In trying to analyze the structure of systems of sounds in various languages previously unknown to me, I learned that I could not do so if I tried to deal exclusively with the sounds themselves. They had to be studied in relation to the grammatical units which they in part comprised (see Pike 1947b). In addition, I needed to study the use of those sounds in relation to the reaction of native speakers (Pike 1947a—as indicated in *Conviction 2.5*). Then, in trying to move to grammatical analysis, I was forced to treat language as a whole, with its grammatical components, in relation to anthropology—to human behavior as a whole (Pike [1954, 1955, 1960] 1967). This problem, in turn, forced me to look more explicitly toward human thought and what turned out to be philosophical presuppositions, even though I did not recognize them as such at the start.

Further Implications: Sinclair (1944:129), for example, affirmed that "explanation does not consist, as we say in a convenient metaphor, in finding 'a reason' for the puzzling fact or situation. It consists in finding a way of regarding a fact or situation so that it is seen as an integral part of a larger whole or system." Compare, also, Margolis (1987:1f) who suggests that a pattern itself becomes part of a feature or subpattern within a larger pattern. Johansson (1989:6f) notes that "holistic views . . . maintain that any particular item can be what it is only if all other items are what they are."

Conviction 5.2. Such a study of patterns within patterns can also be viewed as a type of cohesion (see *Conviction 3.4*), or frame of reference, or system.

Patterns of patterns, within higher patterns, when seen as integrated, suggest that one is approaching some component of truth. A mode of discovery which leads to finding such patterns is not purely formal, but includes the observer, with his physical-social experience, his observer intuition, his observer guesses, and his testing procedures.

Conviction 5.3. Life is in context.

Source: We observe that a baby needs a mother. A plant needs nourishment and water from outside itself. Abstracted meaning needs physical experience as a basis. Structured language form needs language meaning to exist emically. Nothing can survive outside of a patterned context.

Conviction 5.4. Knowledge is related to memory.

Source: A child in school needs to remember what it has been taught; and memory is needed, whether it is at the forefront of conscious knowledge, or whether it is hidden in the person, waiting to be called forth at particular moments for particular purposes. We may call to mind incidents with friends, comments seen on television about history, or folk tales which have been read.

Conviction 5.5. Knowledge of a larger context may tie the particular to the general, or the general to a mass of particulars.

Chapter 5

Source: To live within a society it is not sufficient to know an UNCLE—we must also know his categorized relationship and his relevance within the larger family, or else we may not know how to behave appropriately.

My emic philosophy is complex. It combines observer and thing, thought and act, moral intent and aesthetic judgment. It starts from a complex system, with society and the 'outside' universe integrated in an emic dualism of self and thing. I am encouraged to accept the complexity of my view, however, by the logician Langer ([1937] 1953:185) who says: "If we chance upon a fairly complex and even surprising proposition, from which very many simple ones would follow, we are perfectly justified in taking the former as a postulate and deriving the others from it." And I want my postulates to begin with the ontological, moral, and aesthetic validity of person, and—at least to some degree—with the explanation of things in relation to observers of things who categorize their environments.

With this approach, I can both live 'inside my office' as well as outside it in ordinary behavior.

Conviction 5.6. A person is more than a formal computer. A person needs goals as well as physical form. A person needs pattern of both physical form and mental meaning—and is himself pattern within intersecting patterns.

Source: A person who thinks, only, cannot live. A person who eats, only, cannot live a life of insight in the world. So I start, not with an isolated description of rules, or relations, or classes of items, but with person, thus merging the subjective and the objective in the emics of things and the emics of behavior and the emics of the relation of person to behavior and to things.

Conviction 5.7. In other words, there is no culture apart from an emic structure; no rule apart from an emic structure; no meaning apart from an emic structure; no game apart from an emic structure; no rational behavior apart from emic human beings; no physical form known by us, in itself, apart from our categorizing it emically.

Further Implications: Anthropologist Kearney states (1984:4): "In the short run people's actions are best explained by the ideas they have in their heads. This is the main strategy of cultural anthropology. But in the long run the problem is to explain these ideas, and to do this we must examine the social, economic, political, technological, demographic and geographic conditions in which they developed . . . And here the balance tips in favor of social and material conditions. We can say that this world-view theory is tactically mentalistic, but that strategically it is founded on historical materialism."

The anthropologist Dundes (1968:467) has said that: "For most of the thousands of song and folktale texts recorded in the ethnographic literature, there is either no interpretation at all or else a passing speculative comment or two provided by the collector who tells us what he thinks the song or tale means." And (301): "The formal features of religions, e.g., the techniques of worship or the names and hierarchical ordering of the principal deities, have been dutifully recorded, but too often the underlying or implicit attitudes toward fellow men, toward life, or toward nature in general have not been rigorously investigated. Yet it is essential to know the values of a society if one has any aspirations to understanding that society." Also, in discussing anthropologists as themselves involved in an emic structure or worldview, he notes (1968:150): "There is such a thing as the culture of anthropologists" and (vii) "no human observer can be completely free from his native cultural categories."

Chapter 6

A person may distort innate positive universals into negative particular action.

We know that societies and languages differ radically. How, then, is it possible for us to learn to live comfortably in a different culture? On the other hand, all cultures, all societies and languages, seem to share some kind of activities or goals. Why then do they differ so radically? I like very much the way the philosopher Goodman has stated (1978:x) that "what emerges can perhaps be described as a *radical relativism under rigorous restraints*" [emphasis mine, KLP]. Universal components, innate to all cultures, put restraints on the variability between cultures. Freedom to act to some degree as individuals is also an innate characteristic which allows for diversions.

Conviction 6.1. Nothing really bad is original; the bad is a distortion of the good.

Source: I have developed this conviction recently in a sad attempt to understand continuing international chaos, plus internal difficulties which can be found between some individuals in every culture. If there are exceptions to this conviction, they have not yet come to my attention. The following convictions give some of my current views along this line.

Conviction 6.2. Concerning intellectual universals, one that is present in every society is a desire for wisdom in oneself, or in some of one's respected colleagues. There is a recognition of some degree of wisdom present in any society, with some desire for this to be obtained and utilized by the self.

Concerning the distortion of intellectual universals, the desire for intellectual development can lead negatively to pride in oneself and then, indirectly, to the desire to dominate others in a manner unfortunate for them. From the perspective of others, such knowledge can be looked at negatively, as contributing to objectionable pride.

One source: We may expect to find in every culture some interest in history or in folk tales which emanate from ancestors, along with an expectation that such materials point down the road toward acceptable or successful behavior.

Conviction 6.3. Concerning aesthetic universals, there can be found in every society some kind of approval of materials (or environment) which are considered to be beautiful or pleasing to the eye and ear.

Concerning the distortion of aesthetic universals, negatively, there can be annoyance with, or disapproval expressed about, items which are considered to be ugly or untidy. Every culture, insofar as I know, has criteria which it brings to bear in this way.

Source: I have visited preliterate societies in the Philippines, in Papua New Guinea, in Africa, in South America; in every one I saw evidences of a thirst for beauty. It might be in a painting, or in beautiful earrings, or in the growing of pretty flowers.

Conviction 6.4. Concerning moral universals, there exists in every society some cultural approval of being helped by others, or approval of some kind of personal or social or physical possession or situation being respected and left undamaged or unstolen.

Concerning negative moral universals, theft of some kind or removal of things which are considered to be one's personal or social rights may be disapproved. Among the Mixtec of Mexico, I learned (Pike 1986) that a person could be scolded or ostracized from the community for failure to care for children adequately or for moral delinquency as judged by other members of that community.

Source: I have been astonished at the way in which people in a preliterate society can meet someone from outside that society, who enters with radically different cultural habits, but after some time, can recognize him or her as a *good person* in spite of almost unintelligible (to them) differences of culture. Kindness is a moral universal which is recognizable across vast gaps of appearances and of habit, given time and sufficient contact (before the outsider is killed, for example, under preliminary mistaken evaluation).

Conviction 6.5. Concerning physical or economic universals, every society will have some material which it prizes for food, for shelter, or for other needs. It may have some way for utilizing certain of these for exchange purposes. Hunger will be one physical universal associated with these matters, and there will be some attempt to care for it.

Concerning negative physical or economic universals, integrity in the economic handling of such materials may be downgraded by theft or by cheating in an exchange of goods;

or people may steal, allowing others to die from hunger.

Source: If there were no way to attempt to satisfy hunger, humanity would have died out long ago.

Conviction 6.6. Concerning social universals, people desire some kind of esteem, appreciation, or approval by their society. They want some kind of social structure which allows people to work together, benefit by joint efforts, and to enjoy community fellowship.

Concerning negative social universals, on the other hand, people may be unhappy with some kinds of ostracism, disapproval, or low social classification accorded them within a layer of the society or within cross-layers of the society. They do not want to be rejected, but want to 'belong'.

Source: Again, around the world, we observe not only different ways of living together, but also the constant presence of different ways of giving appreciation or status to individuals in a society.

Conviction 6.7. Concerning alternate but different, affirmed religious universals, every society has members who attempt some explanation, beyond that of the physical, observable features of the society itself or of the nature of the physical world structure. One division here may be viewed as one between a commitment to a theistic accounting for the universe (the path I would follow) or a mechanist one (with a purely physical source of the universe).[13]

Concerning negative religious universals, from the theistic perspective, mechanism could be considered as a negative distortion of reality; from the purely mechanistic perspective, theism might be viewed as a distortion of an academic view of reality. Both views are found in the academic community, with variant perspectives in each.

---

[13] I would call the mechanist approach, from this perspective, a SECULAR RELIGION, as opposed to a THEISTIC RELIGION.

Source: External or internal experiences, including relation to family, society, schooling, research, or unproven starting beliefs (cf. *Conviction 4.2*).

Conviction 6.8. Concerning linguistic universals, I have already pointed out several universal linguistic components around the world: In *Convictions 1:1-2*, the possibility of cross-cultural interaction to language; in *Convictions 1:4-5*, the importance of the naming of emic units, with contrast, variation, and distribution within the units; in *Convictions 3:1-4*, the presence of the three hierarchies of phonology, grammar, and reference, with each of them having different levels of structure, and with tagmemic units on each level of structure, with tagmemic features including slot, class, role, and cohesion; in *Convictions 4:4-6*, the relation of temporary choice of perspective via particle, wave, and field, in terms of the ability of the self to focus in different ways.

Concerning the negation of these linguistic universals, if we were to deny emic units, then no persons, things, or events, could be recognized upon meeting them or seeing them for a second time. If we were to deny hierarchy, life would cease, because one could not tell the difference between a nose and a head, with the part-whole relationship denied. If we were to deny grammar, there could be no structured story, no sentence highlighting a dog which kills versus a dog which gets killed. If we were to deny referential background (horizon, or frame of reference, or social setting), we could never know where we belong in society, nor what happens first, second, or third in a sequence of catastrophic events. If we were to deny a possible choice of focus change from static, to dynamic, to relational views (particle, wave, field) we could never change our attention from doing something to being something.

Source: Observer of human experiences.

Conviction 6.9. Relevance in human language requires simultaneous—or oscillating—attention to both physical form and mental meaning (see also discussion under *Convictions* 2.4–5, 3.3, 4.1–4).

In a phrase such as *goals are important to a good government*, the physical form includes the sounds and the clausal structure, but the referential meaning refers to the structure of government itself, with its values and purposes. Similarly, the noun *goals*, in spite of its abstract referential meaning and implied specific detailed purposes, also has the physical component (its form) of the sounds when it is said aloud, or else—if it is at the moment only a thought in somebody's mind—its formal molecular or neurological structure buried someplace, somehow, in the brain.

Concerning the negation of form or meaning, if we deny the necessity for meaning or for words chosen for their meaning, we may end up with an elegant, logical, theory, but one which is difficult—from my viewpoint—to live with.

Source: My former colleague at the University of Michigan, anthropologist Leslie White, for example, stated (1949:349fn) concerning the "protoplasmic mechanisms that are men" that "whether a man—an average man, typical of his group—'believes in' Christ or Buddha, Genesis or Geology, Determinism or Free Will is not a matter of his own choosing. His philosophy is merely the response of his neuro-sensory-muscular-glandular system to the streams of cultural stimuli impinging upon him from the outside." Similarly, an excessive reliance on the mental factor can lead to hyperboles in another direction. Note the philosopher Katz, who says that he considers preferable the "Platonic realist view that grammars are theories of abstract objects" (1981:3), with "the sentences as abstract objects like numbers" (1981:6).

Conviction 6.10. Contrastive starting points lead to different end results:

Source: The philosopher Searle (1984:55) adopts "a view that does not require us to postulate any intermediate level of algorithmic computational processes mediating between the neurophysiology of the brain and the intentionality of the mind." Since "there is no other level . . . no gap filler is needed between the mind and the brain, because there is no gap to fill." Nevertheless, "we cannot give up our conviction of freedom" (p. 97); and he holds this view in spite of problems of trying to prevent denying any one of the "four features, consciousness, intentionality, subjectivity, and mental causation" which "are what make the mind-body problem seem so difficult" (p. 17). Searle implies that "the features that are characteristic of living beings have a biological explanation" and "exactly similar considerations should apply to our discussions of consciousness" (p. 23). This, in turn, implies to me that Searle holds a belief in the total evolutionary origin of human nature. This makes it difficult for him, it seems to me, to leave a place for a self (or soul) which is sharply divergent from the physical brain and body, even when his own self seems to me to be interacting with it (i.e., with an epistemological fallacy). On the other hand, Searle discusses details of many of the problems involved in any attempt to relate mind and brain much better than I can do.

I would have a different starting point, however, a theistic one which leads to a self or soul of man as beyond that of pure brain and beyond that of a shepherd dog. But just as Searle is unable to explain in detail how he connects believed-in consciousness with a biological source, so I do not know how to try to describe scientifically the nature of the self. Theologians might have something to say in that area, which is beyond my competence; compare, however, treatment by the mathematician-theologian Poythress (1976), of religious assumptions in philosophical relation to particle, wave, and field.

Perhaps it would be appropriate here to give a poem of mine (1985:45f), as (7), which expresses a bit of my own unproven feeling toward the overlapping linkage (and see again 1d).

(7) **Matter and Mind**

> Matter alone will not do.
> Heart will sue
> If neglected.
> > Heart, alone, is sad.
> > Mind, if neglected,
> > Is mad.
>
> 'Nothing but' is death,
> Or hyperbole
> Out of breath.
> > Matter and mind—
> > Tie them up tight,
> > Package them right.

Conclusion

The person in human nature is beyond logic, whether in life, in language, or in philosophy.

Persons can judge emic 'sameness'—which relates personal knowledge to language and experience. Such judgments link the person (as an observer of himself and of his actions in society) to words, to things, to thoughts, and to other people. Persons understand persons and things and events in relation to their occurrence in a significant structural position, in relation to their membership in a class of substitutable items, in relation to their functional role in a social, physical, economic, psychological, and historical structure, and in relation to the control over them exercised implicitly or explicitly by their background frames of reference.

A person can choose unproven starting presuppositions—and may also choose to view a situation or event or thing as if it were for the moment static, dynamic, or relational (particle, wave, field). Such elements are hierarchically arranged in relation to their physical features, or their sequential 'telling' order, or their referential 'happening' order and structure. A person grows in knowledge through the intersection of networks of patterns of patterns of such phonological, grammatical, and referential hierarchies.

A person needs his language to help him know himself in relation to his physical, social, aesthetic, and philosophical environment.

Bibliography

Bien, Joseph, ed. 1978 [1973]. Phenomenology and the social sciences: A dialogue. The Hague: Martinue Nijhoff.

Bruner, Jerome S. 1974 [1972]. The relevance of education. Harmonsworth, Middlesex: Penguin Books.

Catford, J. C. 1965. A linguistic theory of translation: An essay in applied linguistics. London: Oxford University Press.

Dundes, Alan. 1968. Every man his way: Readings in cultural anthropology. Englewood Cliffs: Prentice-Hall.

Einstein, Albert and Leopold Infeld. 1938. The evolution of physics: The growth of ideas from early concept to relativity and quanta. New York: Simon and Schuster.

Flew, Anthony. 1979. A dictionary of philosophy. New York: St Martin's Press.

Frost, S. E. Jr. 1962 revised [1942]. Basic teachings of the great philosophers: A survey of their basic ideas. Garden City: Dolphin Books, Doubleday.

Goodman, Nelson. 1978. Ways of worldmaking. Indianapolis: Hockett Publishing.

Headland, Thomas N., Kenneth L. Pike, and Marvin Harris, eds. 1990. Emics and etics: The insider/outsider debate. Newbury Park: Sage Publications.

Johansson, Ingvar. 1989. Ontological investigations: An inquiry into the categories of nature, man and society. New York: Routledge.

Kant, Immanuel. 1966 [1785]. The fundamental principles of the metaphysic of ethics. In Otto Manthey-Zorn [1938], translator. New York: Appleton-Century-Crofts.

Katz, Jerrold J. 1981. Language and other abstract objects. Totowa, New Jersey: Rowman and Littlefield.

Kearney, Michael. 1984. World view. Novato, CA: Chandler and Sharp.

Lakoff, George. 1987. Women, fire, and dangerous things: What categories reveal about the mind. Chicago: University of Chicago Press.

Langer, Susanne. 1953 [1937]. An introduction to symbolic logic. New York: Dover.

Larson, Mildred L. 1984. Meaning-based translation: A guide to cross-language equivalence. Lanham, MD: University Press of America.

Margolis, Howard. 1987. Patterns, thinking, and cognition: A theory of judgment. Chicago: The University of Chicago Press.

Nida, Eugene A. and Charles R. Tabor. 1969. The theory and practice of translation. Leiden: E. J. Brill.

Ortega y Gasset, Jos. 1985 revised [1952]. ¿Qué es filosofía? Madrid: Alianza Editorial.

Pike, Kenneth L. 1943. Phonetics: A critical analysis of phonetic theory and a technic for the practical description of sounds.

Ann Arbor: The University of Michigan Press.

———. 1947a. Phonemics: A technique for reducing languages to writing. Ann Arbor: University of Michigan Press.

———. 1947b. Grammatical prerequisites to phonemic analysis. Word 3:155–71. Reprinted 1972 in Ruth M. Brend (ed.), Kenneth L. Pike: Selected Writings, 32–50, The Hague: Mouton. Reprinted 1972 in Valerie B. Makkai (ed.), Phonological theory: Evolution and current practice, 153–65, New York: Holt, Rinehart and Winston. Reprinted 1973 in E. C. Fudge (ed.), Phonology: Selected writings, 115–35, Middlesex: Penguin Books.

———. 1959. Language as particle, wave and field. The Texas Quarterly 2:37–54.

———. 1961. Strange dimensions of truth. Christianity Today 5:690–92. Reprinted in Ruth M. Brend (ed.), Kenneth L. Pike: Selected Writings, 301–6, The Hague: Mouton.

———. 1967 [1954, 1955, 1960]. Language in relation to a unified theory of the structure of human behavior. The Hague: Mouton.

———. 1982. Linguistic concepts: An introduction to tagmemics. Lincoln: University of Nebraska Press.

———. 1985. The need for rejection of autonomy in linguistics. The Eleventh LACUS Forum 1984, 35–53, Columbia: Hornbeam.

———. 1986. Mixtec social credit rating—the particular versus the universal in one emic world view. Proceedings of the National Academy of Sciences USA 83: 3047–49.

———. 1988. Bridging language learning, language analysis, and poetry, via experimental syntax. In Deborah Tannen (ed), Linguistics in Context: Connecting observation and understanding. Norwood, NJ: Ablex.

——— and Evelyn G. Pike. 1983. Text and tagmeme. Norwood, NJ: Ablex.

Poythress, Vern S. 1976. Philosophy, science, and the sovereignty of God. Phillipsburg, NJ: Presbyterian and Reformed Company.
Quine, Willard Van Orman. 1960. Word and object. Cambridge: Technology Press of the Massachusetts Institute of Technology.
―――. 1974. The roots of reference. La Salle, IL: Open Court.
――― and J. S. Ullian. 1978. The web of belief. 2nd edition. New York: Random House.
Reeder, Harry P. 1986. The theory and practice of Hussel's phenomenology. Lanham, MD: University Press of America.
Samuel, H. L. 1952. Essay in physics (with a letter from Dr. Albert Einstein). New York: Harcourt Brace.
Searle, John. 1984. Minds, brains and science. Cambridge: Harvard University Press.
Sinclair, Angus. 1944. An introduction to philosophy. London: Oxford University Press.
―――. 1951. The conditions of knowing. London: Rutledge and Kegan Paul.

White, Leslie A. 1949. The science of culture: A study of man and civilization. New York: Farrar Straus.

www.ingramcontent.com/pod-product-compliance
Lightning Source LLC
Chambersburg PA
CBHW051759230426
43670CB00012B/2355